APE
IN A

an alphabet of odd animals

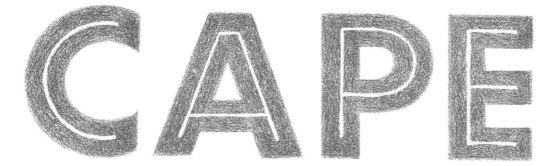

CAPE

by Fritz Eichenberg

HARCOURT, BRACE & WORLD

NEW YORK

Ape in a cape

B Bear in despair

Carp with a harp

D Dove in love

E Egret in a minuet

F Fox in a box

Goat in a boat

H

Hare at the fair

Irish setter with a letter

Jay in May

K

Kitten with a mitten

Lizard with a wizard

M Mouse in a blouse

Nag with a bag

Owl on the prowl

P

Pig in a wig

TRAIL

Q Quail on the trail

R Rat with a bat

Sheep in a leap

T Toad on the road

Unicorn with a horn

Vulture with culture

Whale in a gale

X for Rex

Y

Yak with a pack

Z for zoo

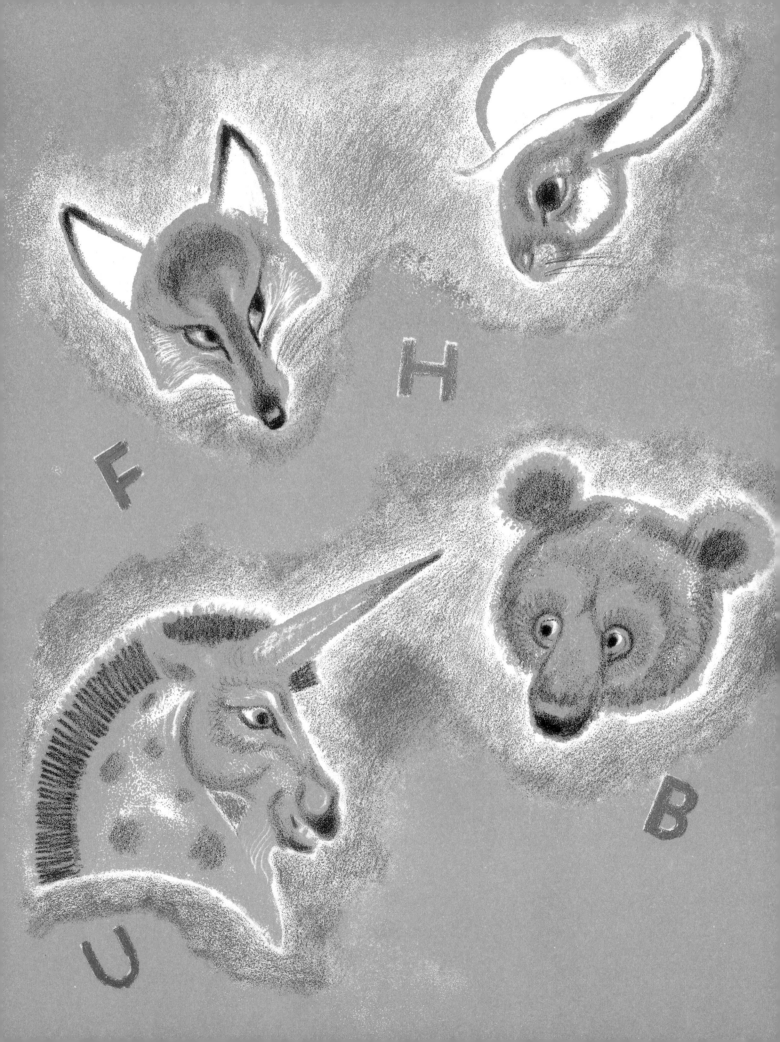